A Sister Is a Very Special Friend

Bestselling Books by

Blue Mountain Press INC.

Books by Susan Polis Schutz:
**To My Daughter, with Love,
on the Important Things in Life
To My Son with Love
Love, Love, Love**

**For You,
Just Because You're Very Special to Me**
by Collin McCarty

**100 Things to Always Remember...
and One Thing to Never Forget**
by Alin Austin

Too Wise to Want to Be Young Again
by Natasha Josefowitz, Ph.D.

Trust in Yourself
by Donna Fargo

Is It Time to Make a Change?
by Deanna Beisser

Chasing Away the Clouds
by Douglas Pagels

Anthologies:
**42 Gifts I'd Like to Give to You
A Sister Is a Very Special Friend
Always Believe in Yourself and Your Dreams
Don't Ever Give Up Your Dreams
For You, My Daughter
I Keep Falling in Love with You
I'll Never Forget the Love That I Shared with You
I Love You, Mom
I Want Our Love to Last Forever
Life Can Be Hard Sometimes... but It's Going to Be Okay
Marriage Is a Promise of Love
Mottos to Live By
Take Each Day One Step at a Time
There Is Greatness Within You, My Son
Thoughts of Love
To My Child
True Friends Always Remain in Each Other's Heart**

A Sister Is a Very Special Friend

A collection of poems
Edited by Robin Andrews

Blue Mountain Press ®

Boulder, Colorado

Library of Congress Catalog Card Number: 91-73571
ISBN: 0-88396-348-5

ACKNOWLEDGMENTS appear on page 62.

 design on book cover is registered in
U.S. Patent and Trademark Office.

Manufactured in the United States of America
First Printing: September, 1991

Blue Mountain Press ®

P.O. Box 4549, Boulder, Colorado 80306

CONTENTS

You Are
the Most Beautiful Person I Know

You are the most beautiful person
I know—
not just outside, but inside, too.
You have a wonderful sense of humor,
a loyalty that not many people have,
and the gift of love you give to others.

We may not be perfect;
we have our share of arguments,
our times of laughter,
and our share of troubles.
Yet we can always trust
one another with anything.

When you just have
to share something,
good or bad,
I will listen.
You are the world to me.
Words can't express my appreciation,
but it means a lot to me
that you are my sister,
and I will love you forever.
A sister like you
is the greatest gift in the world.

—Kristy Jorgensen

What Is a Sister?

A *sister is someone more special than words. She's love mixed with friendship; the best things in life. She's so much inner beauty blended together with an outward appearance that brings a smile to the happiness in your heart.*

A sister is one of the most precious people in the story of your life. And you'll always be together, whether you're near or apart.

Together, you have shared some of the most special moments two people have ever shared. A sister is a perspective on the past, and she's a million favorite memories that will always last. A sister is a photograph that is one of your most treasured possessions. She's a note that arrives on a special day, and when there's news to share, she's the first one you want to call. A sister is a reminder of the blessings that come from closeness. Sharing secrets. Disclosing dreams. Learning about life together.

A sister is a confidante and a counselor. She's a dear and wonderful friend, and—in certain ways— something like a twin. She's a hand within your hand; she's so often the only one who really understands. A sister is honesty and trust enfolded with love. She's sometimes the only person who sees the horizon from your point of view, and she helps you to see things more clearly. She is a helper and a guide, and she is a feeling, deep inside, that makes you wonder what you would ever do without her.

What is a sister? She's someone more special than words; someone beautiful and unique. And in so many ways, there is no one who is loved so dearly.

—Carey Martin

A Sister like You . . .

A sister like you is a special gift . . .
We like to do so many of
the same things, and we share
a lot of wonderful, fun moments.
You respect me for my strengths,
as I admire you for yours.
We encourage each other
during our difficult times,
and laugh with each other
during our good times.
I know I can be myself with you.

A sister like you is a precious gift . . .
We can tell each other
our secret dreams and desires,
cheer each other on to
success and happiness,
and wipe each other's tears
when we are sad and disappointed.
You are a bright light in my life,
and you have a special place in my heart.

I want to wish you all your best
dreams come true,
and that you have success and happiness,
a fulfilled heart, and laughter.
And I want to tell you that
you are beautiful to me,
and I cherish our friendship.

—Donna Levine

A "Thank You"
That Comes from the Heart

You're really something . . .
   do you know that?

You go out of your way
when you don't have to;
you have the ability to
brighten the days
in ways that no one else
   is able to do.
And you really deserve to know
how very much you're appreciated . . .
   because you are.

The special people in this world
really make a difference.

And you, Sister, are definitely
   one of them.

—Collin McCarty

Sister . . .
I want you to know
that I consider our friendship
one of my greatest blessings.
Together, we've built a relationship
that is strong and enduring.
We've consoled each other
and stood by each other.
Our friendship has truly been
a cherished gift,
one that always will remain with us.
I am thankful for all
that we have meant to each other
over the years.
You have touched my life
in so many ways,
and your friendship is something
I will always cherish.

—Deanne Laura Gilbert

You are my sister
and my beautiful lifelong friend.
You listen to my heartaches
and laugh with me
through every joy.
You know me better
than anyone else.
You love me
even when I don't feel
that I deserve it.
You believe in me
when no one else
seems to.
You'll always be
my precious sister
and a special part of me.
I love you.

—Laurel Goff

Sister, I Smile
Whenever I Think of You

*F*or as far back as I can remember,
you've been a special person in my world.
When we were younger,
I was happy simply to have you around
to play with and to share things with.

But over the years, as we grew together,
I began to see you in a different light.
I remember the first time
that we turned to each other for support
and found it.
I remember the first time
that we really confided in one another
and told each other things that
we could not tell anyone else.

I remember crying together,
not as children fighting,
but as friends in need of comfort.
I remember the first time that we hugged,
not because someone told us that we should,
but because we wanted to.

We've grown up.
You aren't just my sister anymore;
you are a friend.
And it seems that the older we grow,
the closer we become.

Yet with this growth
come new opportunities and responsibilities
that often place our worlds farther apart.
I sit here now, as an adult,
appreciating you more than ever,
and a little wave of sadness comes over me.
I miss always having you around.

But I still smile.
After all, my missing you, Sister,
is just another way of saying
I love you.

—Lynn Barnhart

Sister, of All the Friends I've Ever Had . . . You're the Best!

We've had our struggles,
as members of the same family do,
but the love we share
has grown stronger because of them.
You are there for me
when I most need someone.
The things we've shared,
spoken and unspoken,
will always be a bond between us,
no matter where we go.
All our lives, you've understood
and cared more fully
than any friend ever could.
The bonds of family are deep,
and our friendship
brings us together more completely.
The love I have for you,
my wonderful sister,
runs as deep as my love can go.

—Ruthann Tholen

I Believe in You, Sister

I want to tell you that I believe in you;
I believe in your mind
and all the dreams, intelligence,
and determination within you.
You can accomplish anything.
You have so much open to you,
so please don't give up on
      what you want from life
or from yourself.
Please don't put away the dreams
      inside of you.
You have the power to make them real.
You have the power to make yourself
      exactly what you want to be.
Believe in yourself the way I do,
      and nothing will be beyond your reach.

—Joleen K. Fox

There are three
simple wishes
that I hold in my heart
for you.
I wish for you
happiness and special times
for you to enjoy.
I wish for you good health
in everything you do.
But most of all,
I wish for you
the truest love there is
in the world,
and that is the love of family.
I know how much that means to you,
because it will always mean
so much to me.

—Laura Medley

"That's My Sister"

What a treasure to my life she is.
My sister. She's my definition
of love and sweetness
        and understanding
all wrapped up in one
        wonderful person.

She's the best there is. The absolute
best. And I appreciate everything
about her: her beautiful spirit, the
intertwining of our lives, and the way
she brings so many smiles my way.

There will never be a day in my life
when I will not love her, be thankful
for her, admire her, and simply think
about her with a happiness deep
inside me. I'd give anything if she
could know this.

She's someone who means more to me
than she'll ever know.
        That's my sister.
        And what a wonderful
        sister she is.

—Laurel Atherton

Our Friendship Means
Everything in the World to Me

Our friendship means that I have someone
who will drop whatever they're doing
to be with me when I need them.
It means that I have someone I can trust
with my most intimate secrets and thoughts.

Our friendship means that there's
someone I can count on to listen
to my problems and complaints
without judging me.
It means that someone really knows
and understands me
and loves me anyway.

*Our friendship means
that I have a person in my life
who believes in my hopes and dreams
and encourages me to fulfill them.
It means that I have someone
with whom I can share laughter, hugs,
and special times.*

*Our friendship means
that there is someone in this world
who is completely irreplaceable in my life,
who is a loving heart, a companion,
a confidante.
It means that I am among
the lucky few who have a friend
who is part of their very soul.
I have a friend who is
a special, unique,
and essential part of myself:
you, my sister.*

—Barbara Cage

*Through the years, you've been more
than just a sister to me;
you've been a special friend.
I could count on you
to give me a shoulder to cry on,
and you rejoiced in my success.
You stood up for me
even when I didn't deserve your support.
When I didn't believe in myself,
you believed in me and helped me
find the strength and courage to go on.
I've questioned a lot of things
in my life,
but I've never questioned
your love for me.
Somehow, I always knew
it would be there.
I want you to know that,
even though I don't always show it,
I'm glad you're my sister,
and I love you.*

—Judy LeSage

The Understanding We Share Means Everything to Me

*There's so much
more between us
than the shared bond
of family.*

*I can tell my friends
about my life's experiences,
but you understand
in a few words
what it takes me an hour
to explain to someone else.*

We laugh and share our dreams,
and with you I do more
than just hear the words;
I feel the things you feel.
It makes me smile to think
of how the time I spend with you
is what I enjoy
more than almost anything else.

When we talk,
I always come away with a
better understanding of myself and you.
As my sister, you understand me;
as my friend, you accept me.
Sometimes I think that what we have
must be unique in all the world,
and for that I am thankful.

—Katherine Myers

I'll Always Be Your Very Own
Private Cheering Section

*I'll never stop wishing
for the best for you.*

*I'll always be here,
cheering you on, sometimes with
my spoken words, and sometimes
with my silent prayers, and always
with the hope that you will find
happiness on the paths you follow
and success in the days ahead.*

*Your happiness means a lot to me.
And "happy" is something
you deserve to be.*

—Alin Austin

You Will Always Be
My Very Best Friend

We have both gone through
so many changes
over the years,
but one thing has always
remained the same—
we've been the best of friends.
As children we played
side by side together,
creating our childhood dreams
and building our imaginations.
We laughed, shared whispered secrets,
and as the years passed,
we grew together.
As adults, we have shared
our hopes and our dreams.
We've laughed together
about our joys
and cried together over our sorrows.

We've been here for each other
through all aspects of our lives.
No matter what the future
holds for us,
no matter what changes
we may make along the way,
I believe in our relationship
and in our love for each other,
because we're so much more
than family;
we're the best of friends.

—Deanne Laura Gilbert

A Sister like You
Is the Most Special Kind of Friend

You and I share so much more
than the word "friendship"
could ever describe.
You have been an inspiration to me
when I felt that everything
was full of hopelessness.
You have been the force
that brought me back to earth
when I was reaching
for stars so high
that my feet had left the ground.
You have been my guide
as I went through new experiences
in my life.
You have been my light
through any darkness I encountered.
You have been my laughter
when tears seemed my only comfort.
You have been the inspiration
behind so many of my smiles.
You are so much more
than a friend;
you are my sister,
and I love you.

—Penny-Jean

*Sister, I just want you to know
how much I think about you
and how wonderful I feel
  to have you for my sister.*

*You are like a part of me,
and even when we aren't together,
  I feel that we are united by an
    unbreakable bond.*

No one understands us like we do.
No one has shared the same memories;
no one else knows all of the problems,
joys, and secrets we've shared.
Our love is stronger than anything
that has or will ever come between us.
You fill my life
with smiles and laughter,
*   consolation and understanding.*

Thank you for being both a special
sister and a wonderful friend.
May the future hold the same closeness
and enthusiasm that we share today,
and may this bond of love
and friendship continue to be
a source of strength
and comfort for both of us.

—Barbara Cage

I'm Always Here for You

Whenever you go through
the really tough times in your life,
I want you to know that
my thoughts and prayers are with you.
It hurts me to see you hurting,
and I wish I could make things
better for you with a word or a hug.
But all I can do is tell you
that I really do care about you
far more than you'll ever know.
I want your life to be everything
you wish it to be,
so hang in there and keep trying.
Things will get better with time.
Always remember that you mean
much more to me than I can say,
and I'm here for you
if you ever need me.
I love you, my sister.

—Deanne Laura Gilbert

Sister,
the Miles Will Never
Come Between Us

There is a special closeness
  that we share.
I can remember our younger days,
when we were able to share
so many things in our life,
but as we grew older,
it was hard to spend as much
time together as we once did.
There are so many miles
  between us now
that we don't get the chance
to visit as much
  as we would like to.

Yet, after all these years
and all these miles,
you are as close to me
  as you were before.
I miss the long talks
we used to have,
I miss seeing you,
I miss spending time together.
Although the miles have become
an obstacle for us,
they will not be able to
  come between us,
because my love for you
and the closeness we share
will overcome
any distance in our way.

—Francine A. Gabriel

I'm Glad We
Are Always There
for Each Other

I know I don't tell you very often
how happy I am that we're family.
But I want you to know that
even though we have our differences
and misunderstandings,
there are always smiles, laughter,
and love to remind me
of just how much you mean to me.
We have a special bond
that holds us together through life,
even though we find it hard
to sometimes admit it.
But I know that no matter what,
you will always be there for me.
I hope that you know, too,
that whenever you need me,
and for whatever reason,
I'll always be here for you.

—Mary M. Zappone

Life with You, Sister,
Has Always Been Wonderful

*B*eing family means more
than growing up in the same house,
having the same relatives,
or even sharing the same last name.
But by living in the same house
and sharing with each other
everything else we have in common,
we were given a great opportunity
to get to know each other
as well as we do.
Being family means being us:
  you and me.
It's true that chance brought us
together,
but it was by our own choice
that we've become such close friends.

*We've seen each other
through some thrilling moments
and some troublesome ones, as well.
You are always the first person
I think of when I want to share,
or if I just need a special person
to confide in.
You've always had the ability
to look objectively at the situation,
yet you also make me feel as if
my happiness is all that matters.
For as long as I have known you,
I've considered myself very lucky
to have found in you
both a sister and a friend.
I would like to thank you for
touching my life
and for inspiring me
in the many ways that you do.*

—Mary Kunz

We Will Always Share
Something Special

As the years pass by us,
no matter how much we change,
I will still hold within me
those times that were ours alone
when we were growing up.
As we grow older
and time changes us,
whether we're busy with families
    or careers,
I know we will continue
to share secrets
and take time to talk
    and find some smiles.

For no matter how much
    time passes,
we will remember and hold
    inside of us
the special bond
that only we can share.

—Pamela Schuster

Sister, I'm Grateful for
Our Closeness

*I always think about you
in a loving way,
because you have always been
so special to me.
The love I have for you as my sister
is something
I was born into,
but the love I have
for you as a person
is something that came
from your thoughtful, giving heart,
your warm, loving ways,
and your total honesty.
I have been blessed to have you
as a sister.*

*Growing up was
an adventure we shared
that I will always cherish.
Having you as a friend
has allowed me to know there is someone
who really cares what happens to me,
    someone I can depend on,
someone who knows me and loves me
for what I am and what I will become.*

*Thank you, my sister, for the closeness
    we share.*

—Patricia L. Kirchner

You Are . . .

You're one of the dearest and most
treasured people in my world.
You're my reminder to never
    lose hope and to always find
    a reason to smile. You're sweet
and wonderful and precious to me.
And you're the inspiration behind
so much of the laughter and so much
of the love that have blessed my life.
    There's no one else
    as special to me . . . as you . . .

Because you're all that . . .

    and you're my sister, too.

—Chris Gallatin

I'm Glad We've Become
Such Good Friends Through the Years

Growing up together
was not always easy.
I just did not understand
the significance of it—
maybe because I did not
get to pick you out,
like I did my friends.
I look back on those days
and it makes me wonder
why we were not
just a little closer.
As time passed,
friends pulled us apart
and we drifted for a while,
taking separate paths
until one day
we felt the strength
of the age-old bond
between us.

It's hard to imagine
my life, my secrets,
without thinking of you
and feeling your open warmth.
I know that we have
a lot in common
that brings us together
as a family,
but there is more than that—
there is the bond of friendship,
of trusting, caring, being there,
of knowing our childhood memories
were created together.
I look back on the friends
that I chose long ago
and I wonder what
I was looking for,
because the best friend
I could ever have had
was always right beside me.
I love you, my sister, my friend.

—Beth Fagan Quinn

We have shared so many experiences
throughout our lives,
and I know that there will be many more
in the years to come—
moments that only family
and the closest of friends can share.

I hope that you can always feel
how very much I love you,
not just because we are related,
but because of the real connection
we have that stems from our hearts.
You are a wonderful person,
a great sister,
and I love you.

—Donna Newman

I Don't Know What I'd Do Without You

For keeping my spirits up.
For never letting me down.
For being here for me.
For knowing I'm there for you.

For bringing so many smiles my way.
For being sensitive to my needs.
For knowing just what to say.
For listening better than anyone else.

For bringing me laughter.
For bringing me light.
For understanding so much about me.
For trusting me with so much about you.

For being the best.
For being so beautiful.

   I don't know what I'd do
    . . . without you.

—Collin McCarty

We Share a Special Bond of Love

*Being family means
sharing a lot of things
throughout life.
It means knowing certain things
about each other
and feeling special feelings
for one another.
It is a relationship
we have seen change with time,
and yet, in many ways,
it remains the same.
I know there have been times
when being family wasn't easy,
because our differences
pulled us in new directions.
But we always knew
that we cared about one another.
That's the beautiful part
of being who we are.
Even though life is full of changes,
we will always have each other,
and we will always share
a special bond of love.*

—Laura Medley

Sister, You Have
a Special Place in My Heart

*There is never a time in my life
when I'm not with you in some way.
There are moments
when you come to my mind more strongly,
sometimes in a special way,
but you are with me always.
Sometimes you are with me
in the warm memory
of some laughter we've shared.*

I admire your personality,
your character, and the qualities you possess.
You are a capable and determined person.
There is an understanding we have developed,
a relationship that shows we care,
and a oneness that has grown
out of respect, patience, and love.
If I could give you
the happiness and success that you deserve,
it would last forever.
I wish you all that you desire
and all that is beautiful.
You will forever be a part of me and my life,
because you have a place in my heart.
I love you, Sister.

—*Victor Barbella*

ACKNOWLEDGMENTS

The following is a partial list of authors whom the publisher especially wishes to thank for permission to reprint their works.

Ruthann Tholen for "Sister, of All the Friends . . ." Copyright © 1991 by Ruthann Tholen. All rights reserved. Reprinted by permission.

Judy LeSage for "Through the years, you've been . . ." Copyright © 1991 by Judy LeSage. All rights reserved. Reprinted by permission.

Katherine Myers for "The Understanding We Share . . ." Copyright © 1991 by Katherine Myers. All rights reserved. Reprinted by permission.

Deanne Laura Gilbert for "You Will Always Be My Very Best Friend" and "I'm Always Here for You." Copyright © 1991 by Deanne Laura Gilbert. All rights reserved. Reprinted by permission.

Penny-Jean for "A Sister like You Is . . ." Copyright © 1991 by Penny-Jean. All rights reserved. Reprinted by permission.

Francine A. Gabriel for "Sister, the Miles Will Never . . ." Copyright © 1991 by Francine A. Gabriel. All rights reserved. Reprinted by permission.

Mary M. Zappone for "I'm Glad We Are Always There . . ." Copyright © 1991 by Mary M. Zappone. All rights reserved. Reprinted by permission.

Patricia L. Kirchner for "Sister, I'm Grateful for Our Closeness." Copyright © 1991 by Patricia L. Kirchner. All rights reserved. Reprinted by permission.

A careful effort has been made to trace the ownership of poems used in this anthology in order to obtain permission to reprint copyrighted materials and to give proper credit to the copyright owners. If any error or omission has occurred, it is completely inadvertent, and we would like to make corrections in future editions provided that written notification is made to the publisher:

BLUE MOUNTAIN PRESS, INC., P.O. Box 4549, Boulder, Colorado 80306.